Sussex and t

Armada

JEREMY GORING

PASTFINDER PUBLICATIONS
Lewes

First published by Pastfinder Publications
31 Houndean Rise, Lewes BN7 1EQ

ISBN 1 871301 00 9

Set in 11pt Baskerville by AB Composer Typesetters
14 Mount Street, Lewes BN7 1HL

Printed by Laceys (Printers) Ltd
196 Old Shoreham Road, Hove BN3 7EH

Plates

Maps

Front cover: The Spanish Armada off the coast of Sussex from an engraving by John Pine (1739), based on an Elizabethan tapestry in the House of Lords.

'Look well to the coast of Sussex', warned Sir Francis Drake in 1587 on his return from his expedition to Cadiz to 'singe the King of Spain's beard' by obstructing the preparations for the Armada.[1] In fact the English government did not need to be reminded that the Sussex coast was exceptionally vulnerable to enemy attack. Earlier in the century, when England was at war with France, there had been two major incursions—one in 1514, when the enemy had burned Brighton, and another in 1545, when they had landed a large army at Seaford.[2] At that time Sussex, with its long and exposed coastline, was said to be 'the place of most danger within this realm'.[3] Now that the threat came from Spain the most dangerous place was probably Kent, whose coast lay uncomfortably close to the Spanish Netherlands; but there was always a real possibility of a secondary assault upon Sussex.

So it was that in 1585, when news reached England of the Spanish King's hostile intentions, Lord Howard of Effingham, Lord Admiral of England, was appointed Lord Lieutenant of Sussex and Surrey and ordered to make urgent preparations for coastal defence. In the following year he was joined in his commission by Thomas Sackville, Lord Buckhurst, a cousin of the Queen and a prominent member of her Privy Council, whose country home was at Withyham. Since Howard was pre-occupied with his naval duties Buckhurst was effectively in sole command of the shire, although he left much of the work of organising the militia to his three Deputy Lieutenants, Sir Thomas Palmer of Angmering, Walter Covert of Slaugham and Nicholas Parker of Willingdon.

In theory the 'militia' comprised all the able-bodied male inhabitants aged between 16 and 60, who were supposed to hold themselves in readiness to come to the defence of the shire at an hour's warning, equipped with whatever arms and armour they could lay hands on. Of these a small proportion had been organised into 'trained bands': Sussex was supposed to have 2000 'trained men'—800 with firearms and the rest armed with bills, pikes or bows and arrows—but, in view of the county's notorious slackness in fulfilling its military obligations, the actual numbers were almost certainly lower.[4] Pitting such a puny force against the armed might of Spain would have been as hazardous as putting the Home Guard into action against the Germans in the Second World War: in neither case would 'Dad's Army' have been a match for the best-trained and best-equipped army in Europe.

In the late summer of 1586, before Buckhurst had had time to do

SUSSEX IN 1587

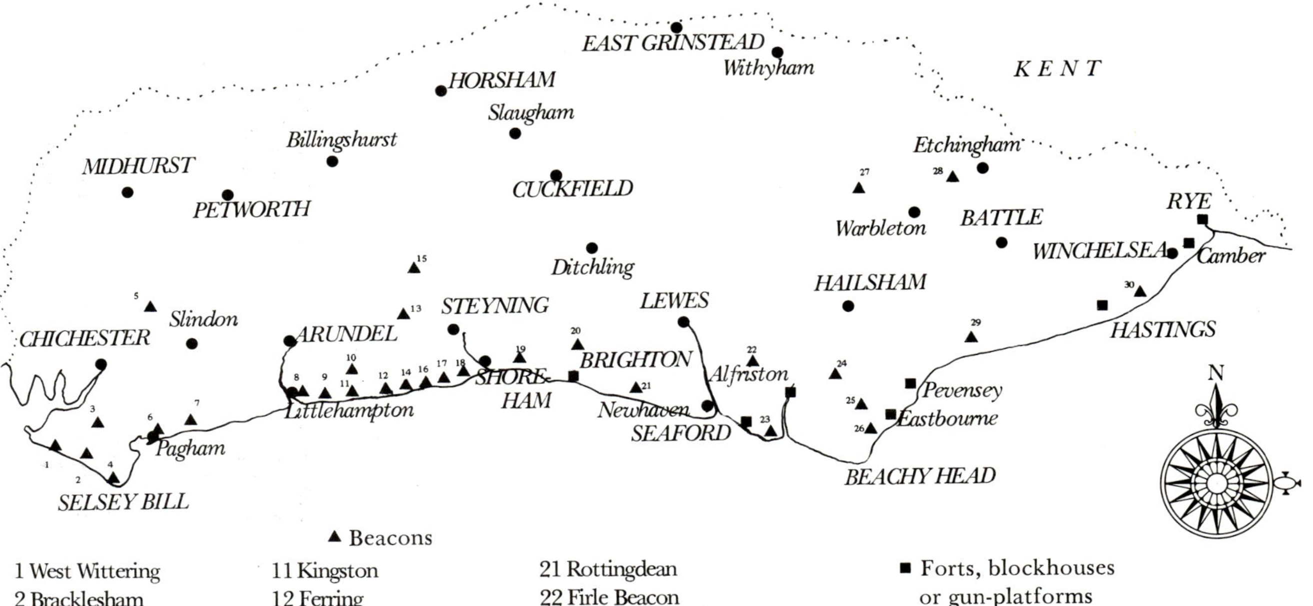

▲ Beacons

1 West Wittering
2 Bracklesham
3 Selsey
4 Sidlesham
5 The Trundle
6 Pagham
7 Felpham
8 Littlehampton
9 Preston
10 Highdown
11 Kingston
12 Ferring
13 Cissbury Ring
14 Goring
15 Chanctonbury Ring
16 Heene Mill
17 Worthing
18 Lancing
19 Aldrington
20 Brighton
21 Rottingdean
22 Firle Beacon
23 Seaford
24 Wilmington
25 Willingdon
26 Eastbourne
27 Cross-in-Hand
28 Burwash
29 Cooden Down
30 Fairlight

■ Forts, blockhouses or gun-platforms

0 10 miles
10 km.

much about the training and equipping of the militia, there was a major invasion scare: fifty strange ships were sighted 'hovering to and fro' off Brighton. A messenger from the town, 'adding ten to the number and bringing word that threescore ships were descried', brought the news to Buckhurst, who promptly assembled about 1600 men and camped out with them all night on the Downs between Brighton and Rottingdean. Next day further reinforcements hurried to the scene from all over Sussex, while the men of west Kent, evidently alarmed by a beacon fired (by mistake) at Burwash, were also preparing to march. Word had it that two vessels had come close in shore and had fired salvoes in the direction of Saltdean, but fortunately the rumour proved false. Eventually it transpired that the ships were Dutch merchantmen bound for Holland from Spain and they had come close in shore 'only to get the wind'.[5]

Next summer a hostile fleet was again reported to be sailing up channel and Howard urged Palmer, the resident Deputy Lieutenant in west Sussex, to 'let good care be had towards Arundel'. He ordered him to position horsemen at various points along the coast 'that with speed may give warning' of any invasion and

> If there be any offering to land you shall do well to get as many pioneers as you can and to cut trenches and there to lay your shot to impeach their landing.

Once more the rumours were unfounded and Palmer and his colleagues were able to get on with their preparations in a calm and collected manner.[6]

Their main task that year (1587) was to survey the whole coast of Sussex and make a map showing 'what places of descent be most dangerous for enemies to land at'. Happily their map survives. It shows that the entire stretch of shore from West Wittering to Brighton (with the exception of a rocky stretch between Pagham and Littlehampton) offered 'good landings' to the enemy and that trenches needed to be dug at the most exposed places: apparently none existed anywhere except at Whitehawk Hill near Brighton. From Brighton to Beachy Head the cliffs and rocks would generally prevent a landing, but there were one or two vulnerable spots: it was thought that trenches should be dug at Saltdean and that Birling Gap should be 'rammed up'; more substantial earthworks were needed at Newhaven, Cuckmere Haven and East Blatchington where, it was noted, 'an entry was made by the French'. To the east of Beachy Head the coast between Eastbourne and Fairlight would afford an enemy a 'good landing upon the beach', but progress inland would be impeded by marsh or (beyond Hastings) by cliffs; however a 'rampire' was recommended at Bulverhithe, while Pevensey Castle was 'to be re-edified or utterly razed'. Little was said about the coast beyond Fairlight but there was reassuring news about Camber Castle, built in Henry VIII's reign and subsequently allowed to decay: the castle was now reported to be 'in good repair' and 'well furnished with ordnance and munition'. Generally speaking there was a great shortage of guns and ammunition: apart from Camber the only places with adequate firepower were Brighton, Hastings, Rye and (surprisingly) Alfriston, where '2 pieces mounted and furnished' had been positioned near the church. The surveyors were particularly worried because there was no artillery whatsoever between Brighton and Shoreham: they suggested that two heavy guns and two lighter ones be 'kept in some good house' there, 'to be ready at sudden'.[7]

The map also marks the positions of all the beacons near the coast. Most of them were doubtless ancient sites, for beacons had formed an essential feature of England's 'early warning system' since the fourteenth century. Those sited just to the north of Brighton in 1587 appear to have been in the same place as those depicted in the drawing of the French attack on the town in 1514. The orders for the maintenance of the beacons issued in 1585 expressly stated that they were to be in 'the accustomed places'. What was new about these orders was the tightness of the regulations regarding the watching of the beacons: five householders were to oversee each pair of beacons and were to ensure that two of their number were always at home 'to attend that service' if need arose.[8] This was an onerous duty and in November 1585 Howard acceded to his deputies' request that beacon-watching be suspended in the winter months; but a year later the Privy Council insisted that coastal beacons be watched throughout the winter—and this remained the rule until 1588.[9]

Early in January 1588 the Privy Council, by now very anxious about the 'great preparations of shipping and men' going on in Spain and fearful that, in the event of an invasion of Spanish Catholics intent on the re-conversion of England, their English co-religionists would rally to their aid, ordered Buckhurst to round up the leading Sussex recusants and place them in the care of reliable clergy and gentlemen—or, if this proved impossible, to have them locked up in common gaols. Buckhurst, a sensitive man who could not bring himself to regard recusants as traitors, found the task distasteful: on one

Pl.I. Camber Castle, the strongest bulwark on the Sussex coast.

Pl.II. Alfriston Church, site of an Elizabethan gun platform.

occasion he rebuked his deputies for proposing to imprison a leading Catholic, Anthony Kempe of Slindon, before his case had had a fair hearing. Nevertheless numerous recusants were interned and, in some cases, were to remain so until long after the Armada had come and gone.[10]

The task of rounding up recusants may have distracted the Deputy Lieutenants from their main work of mustering the armed force of the shire; for early in April the Privy Council wrote to express surprise and displeasure that so little had been done in Sussex to get ready for the coming of the Armada. Buckhurst was in the embarrassing position of being a signatory to the Council's letter, which was addressed to Howard and himself but of which, since Howard was at sea, he was the sole recipient. The letter reached him at his London house at 9 p.m. on 3 April and he lost no time in implementing its instructions. He sat down at once to write to his deputies, pointing out that Sussex was apparently the only shire in England that had failed to return the required muster certificates and urging them to swift action; and before 10 p.m. he had despatched the letter by a footman to his 'cousin Parker' at Lewes.[11] Naturally he sent the letter to Lewes: the town, strategically situated 'in the middle of the shire', was (as he put it) the 'most fittest' in Sussex to serve as a military and administrative headquarters. Here was located the county's arsenal of guns and ammunition: six pieces of cast iron ordnance, six 'carriages' and nine pairs of wheels for the ordnance, 42 barrels of gunpowder and 120 cast iron shot. Significantly Buckhurst himself had recently bought a house in the town—'The Vyne', now 'Shelley's Hotel'—and from here, later in the year, he was to superintend the defence of the shire.[12]

In the meantime his colleague Howard was busy gathering a fleet of ships with which to engage the Spanish at sea; and to this the Sussex ports had been required to make a contribution. After some protestations about their poverty the inhabitants of the largest port, Rye, had eventually agreed that (with the help of Tenterden, their 'limb') they could manage to provide one ship. This ship, the *William*, had been hired from a French privateer and may already have been well armed before the townsmen supplied her with four guns from their store. She carried a crew of 59, including William Coxson as captain, Edward Beale as master and Matthew Flory—a prominent member of the French Protestant community in Rye—as surgeon. She was amply provisioned: on board there were 14 tuns of beer, 300

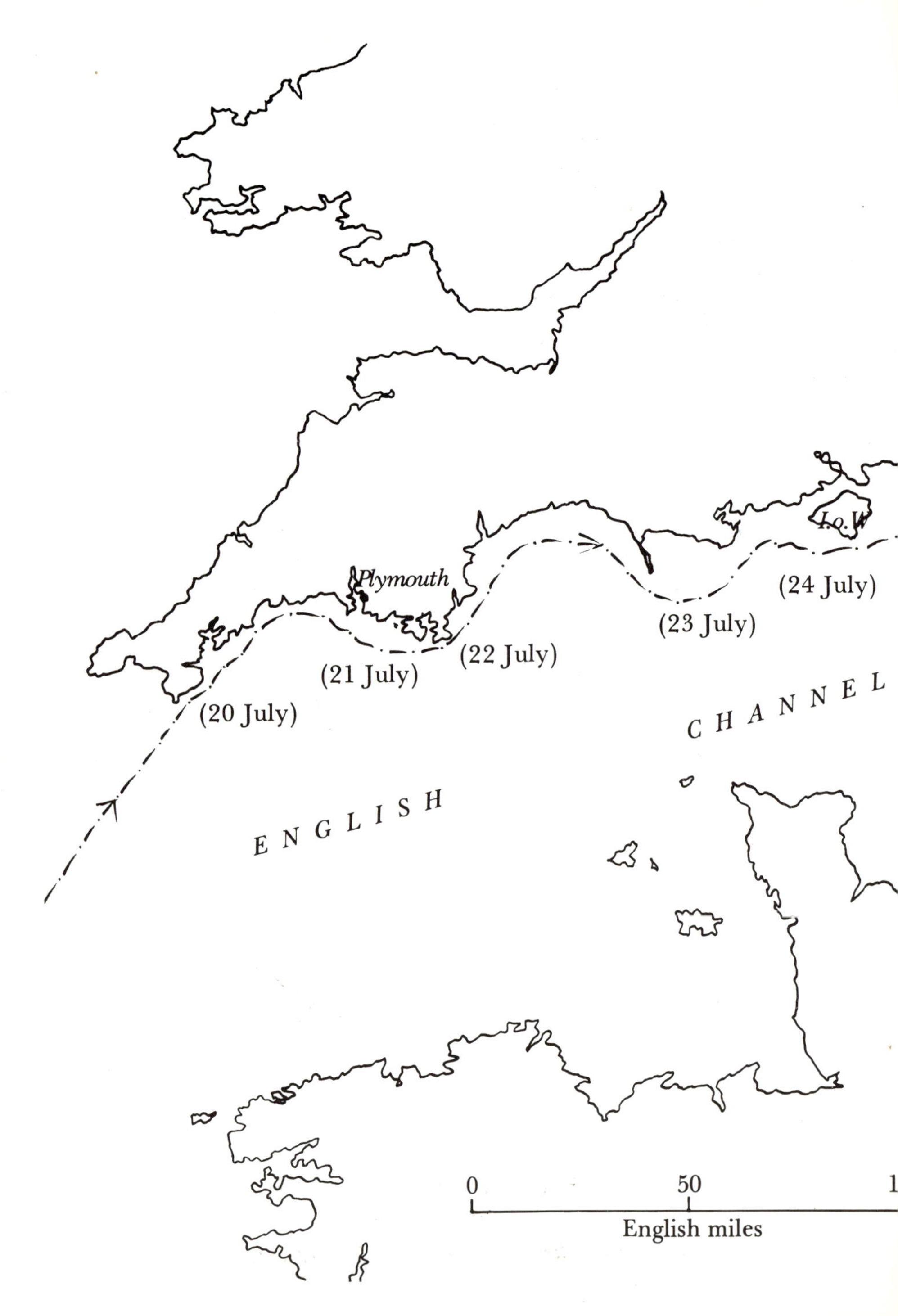
Plymouth
I.o.W.
(20 July)
(21 July)
(22 July)
(23 July)
(24 July)
ENGLISH
CHANNEL
0
50
English miles

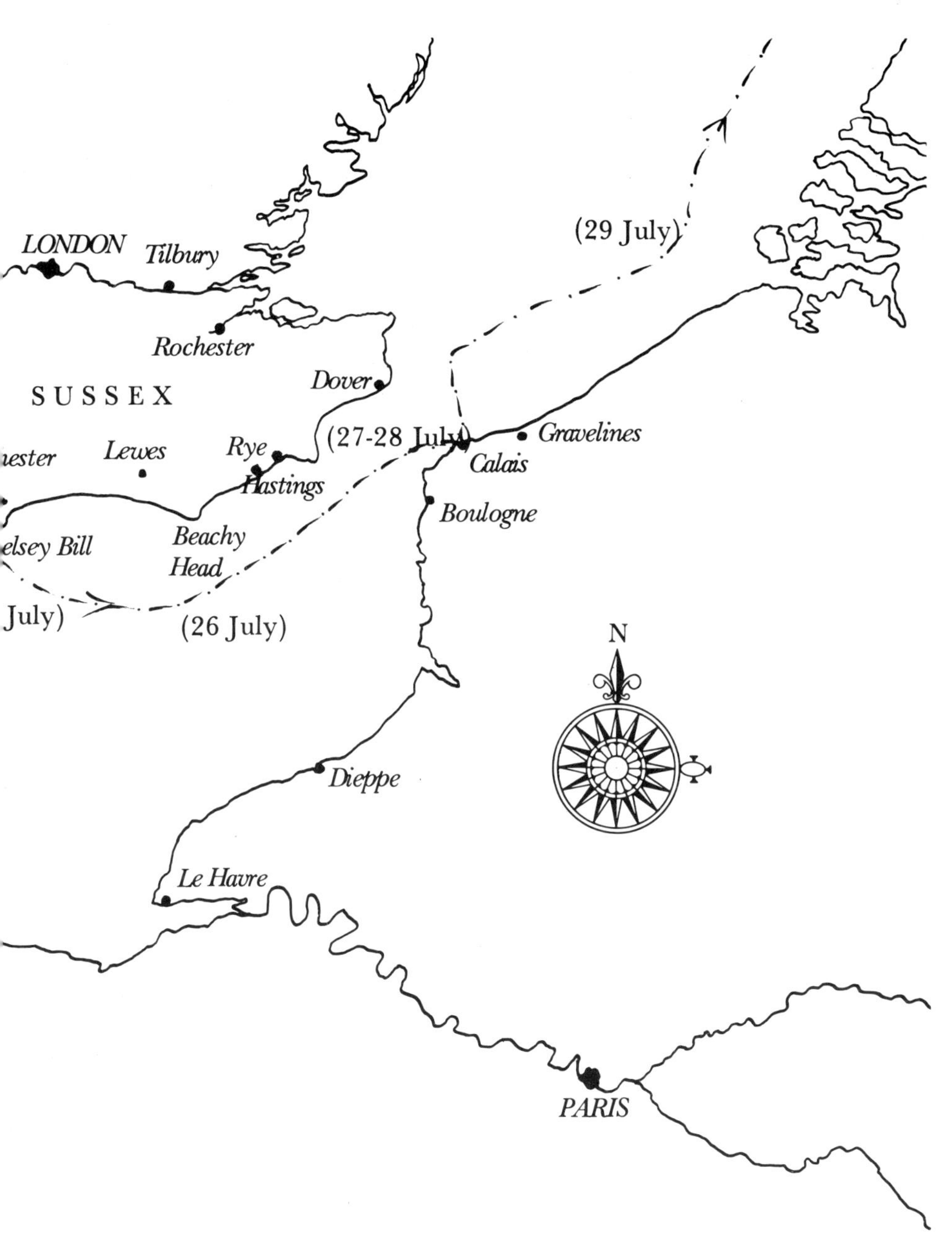

THE COURSE OF THE SPANISH ARMADA
20-29 July 1588
According to Old Style Calendar (see footnote 17)

nails of beef, 100 saltfish, 2 cwt. of bacon, 1 cwt. of butter, 1 cwt. of cheese, one seam of peas and 2,500 biscuits, 'with oatmeal, mustard, candles and such like necessaries'.[13] By the beginning of May the *William* was ready to sail, in company with a second ship, the *Anne Bonaventure*, supplied by Hastings with assistance from Winchelsea.[14] Originally there was to have been a third ship, jointly provided by Chichester, Arundel, Shoreham, Brighton and Lewes—Sussex ports lying outside the Cinque Ports federation—but, after they had protested that 'they had no convenient ship', they were released from their obligation. In the end it was arranged that a vessel should be provided by the Lord Admiral and the charges borne jointly by the five towns and the inhabitants of the six rapes of the shire.[15]

Besides the crews of these three vessels hundreds of other mariners were recruited in Sussex to serve in the fleet at the Crown's charge. This caused some places to become so denuded of able-bodied men that people feared for their safety in the event of invasion. The men of Hastings complained to the Privy Council about 'the weakness of the town', since 'so many mariners, of whom the inhabitants do chiefly consist, are gone to the sea to the Lord Admiral'. The Council wrote back to remind them that 'the strength of Her Majesty's navy is their defence', but added by way of reassurance that they would ask Buckhurst to ensure that the men of the adjoining hundreds were ready to come to their aid in case of need.[16]

By the time the Sussex ships and the rest of Howard's fleet reached Plymouth (on 23 May) the Armada had already set sail. This magnificent fleet of 130 ships, carrying 22,000 combatants, 180 priests and friars, and (allegedly) 123,790 cannon balls, had begun to work its way out of Lisbon harbour on 18 May and two days later was on course for England.[17] But in England no one yet knew this: not until early July did Howard receive definite intelligence that the Armada had sailed and, having been badly mauled by storms, had taken shelter at Corunna. Meanwhile, as Howard's fleet lay at Plymouth, watching and waiting for the Armada's arrival, back in Sussex there seems to have been remarkably little activity. Apparently it was not until the second week in July, when the Spanish fleet—now reduced to some 70 ships—was setting sail from Corunna on the last lap of the voyage to England, that Buckhurst took up residence in Lewes and began the huge task of mustering the shire. On 21 July, when the Armada was already off the coast of Cornwall, the two professional soldiers sent into Sussex to act as muster-masters penned a report to Walsingham,

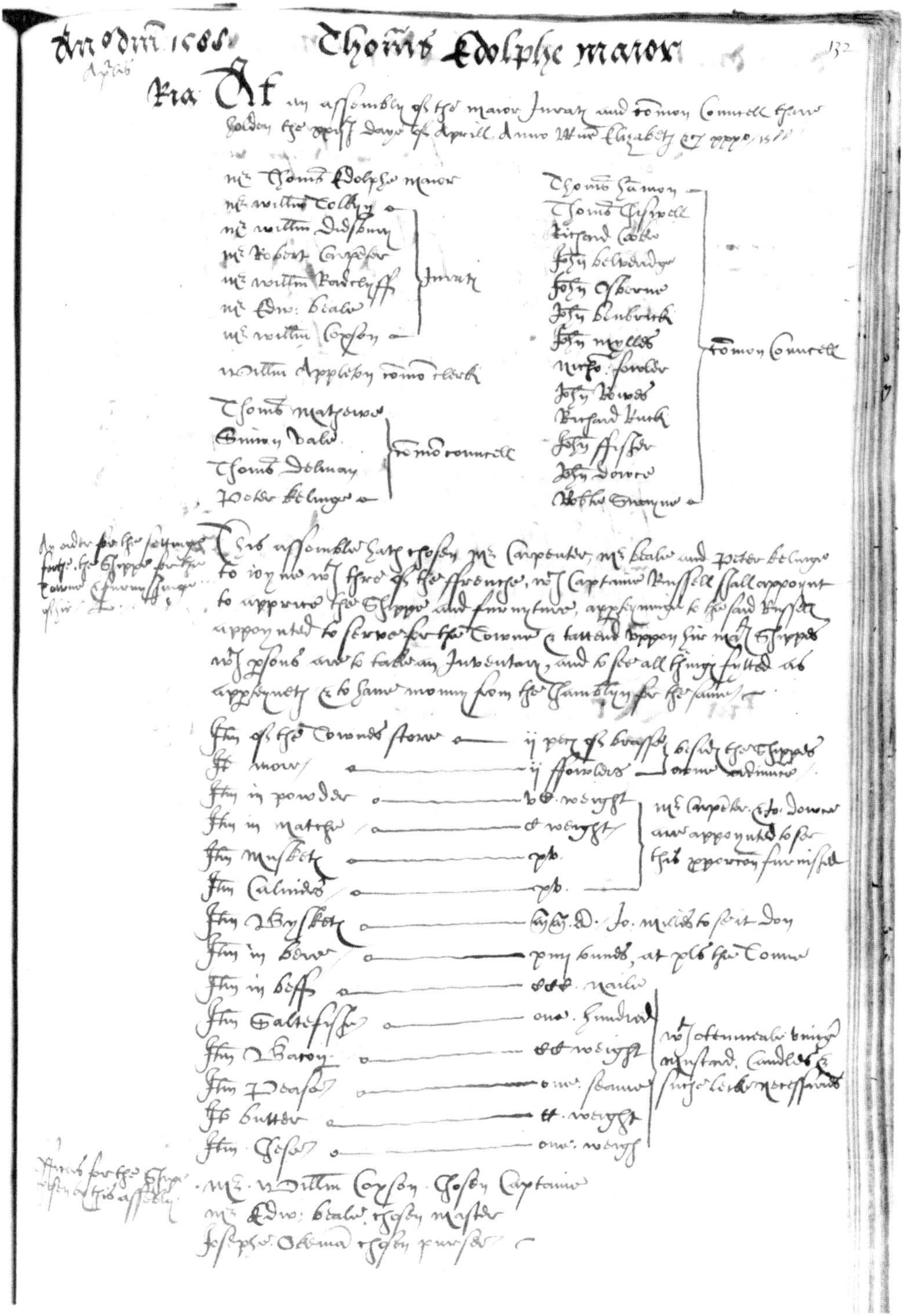

Anno dni 1588 Thomas Edolphe maior

Rya At an assembly of the maior Jurats and comon Councell there holden the xvj daye of Aprill Anno Rne Elizabeth xxx 1588

Mr Thomas Edolphe maior
Mr William Colbye, Mr William Didsbury, Mr Robert Carpenter, Mr William Radcliff, Mr Edw: Beale, Mr William Coxson — Jurats
William Appleby comon clerk
Thomas Matthewe, Henry Dale, Thomas Dolman, Peter Bellinger — comon councell
Thomas Hamon, Thomas Chiswell, Richard Cooke, John Bellingham, John Osborne, John Benbrick, John Mellowe, Nicho: Fowler, John Bowes, Richard Burch, John Fisher, John Dowre, Robert [illegible] — comon Councell

An order for the setting forth the Shippe for the Towne [illegible]

This assemblie hath chosen Mr Carpenter, Mr Beale and Peter Bellinger to joyne with those of the Strangers, which Captaine Russell shall appoint to oversee the Shippe and furnyture, appertayninge to the said Russell appointed to serve for the Towne & take upon him the Shippe with persons and to take an Inventary, and to see all things fitted as appertayneth & to have money from the Chamberlyn for the same.

Item of the Townes store — ij peces of brasse
It more — ij fowlers — beside the Shipps owne ordinaunce
Item in powder — lxx weight
Item in matche — c weight
Item Musketts — xx
Item Calivers — xx — Mr Carpenter & Jo. Dowre are appointed to see this provision furnished
Item Byskett — [illegible] Jo. Mellowe to sett downe
Item in Bere — xxiij tonnes, at cost of the Towne
Item in beefe — ccc [illegible]
Item Saltfyshe — one hundred
Item Bacon — cc weight
Item Pease — one [illegible]
Item butter — c weight
Item Chese — one weight — with other necessarie things [illegible], candles & such like necessaries

Officers for the Shipp chosen by this assemblie
Mr William Coxson chosen Captaine
Mr Edw: Beale chosen Master
Joseph Osborne chosen purser

Pl.III. *'An Order for the setting forth of the Ship from the Town', Rye Corporation register, 1588.*

Pl.IV. Making Peace with Spain, Somerset House, 1604. (Buckhurst, now Earl of Dorset, sits next to the window on the right, with Howard of Effingham, now Earl of Nottingham, on his left. The 6-man Spanish delegation face them across the table.)

the Secretary of State, that must have made his hair stand on end. They informed him that, although Lord Buckhurst had 'put himself to exceeding pains and travels' in supervising the work, he had so far managed to muster only half the shire: three out of six rapes had yet to be reviewed. Even more alarming was the muster-masters' report on the state of the soldiery: the 'trained soldiers' turned out to be men 'utterly untrained by any man of experience', so that 'without further training they will hardly be able to perform any service'. In the circumstances all that they could do was 'to teach and train them in such wise as the present shortness of time would suffer'. The Lord Lieutenant, they said, planned to make better arrangements in future but, with the Spanish fleet only a few days away, that could hardly have given Walsingham much consolation.[18]

On 24 July, when the Armada was off the Isle of Wight, the Council wrote to Buckhurst, then presumably still in the throes of mustering the shire, to tell him that, although it was now unlikely that the Spaniards would try to invade Sussex, he was nevertheless to see the militia 'disposed in apt and convenient places throughout the shire'.[19] Two days later they wrote again to say that the Armada 'will shortly be upon the coast of Sussex' and that he was to supply Howard, who was pursuing them, with all the additional men and munitions he required.[20] It was in fact on 25 July that the Spanish fleet first came in sight of the Sussex coast: it came so close, moreover, that it nearly foundered on the deadly Owers rocks off Selsey Bill. Thereafter it stood off to the south-south-east and, to the great relief of the Lord Admiral (who knew better than anyone else afloat the true state of things in Sussex), it kept well clear of the coast. And so when, as the Lewes 'Town Book' prosaically records, 'the Spanish fleet came along by Newhaven', it may have been so far out to sea as to be invisible even to a look-out on the keep of Lewes castle. It was at this time (probably 26 July) that the Lewes constables handed over 20 barrels of gunpowder in their custody 'unto the use of the Right Honourable Lord Buckhurst. . . for my Lord Admiral', who by then was desperately short of powder and shot.[21] The barrels were doubtless taken down the Ouse to one of Howard's supply vessels lying off Newhaven.

On 31 July Buckhurst, who was still at Lewes, wrote to the captains within the shire to tell them the good news that the immediate danger was past. They were therefore to dismiss the men lately appointed to guard the coast, ordering them 'upon pain of death' to be ready to return at an hour's warning; beacons were to be maintained with double watch; 'watch and ward' was still to be kept in all 'thoroughfare towns' and at the main bridges and crossroads; and innkeepers were to 'mark what bruits and rumours are given forth'. But the most important instructions were left to the last: because the enemy 'bendeth all his force towards the Thames and the coast of Kent' the 2000 men of the trained bands already on stand-by and 500 additional men were to be sent to Croydon by 9 August.[22] The men were to serve under Sir Thomas Shirley of Wiston, who was now 'colonel' in the army to be assembled under the Earl of Leicester at Tilbury. Significantly the companies of footmen were to be placed under the command of 'captains of skill and experience', who were to replace the 'country captains' whose lack of skill and experience had been shown up at the recent musters.[23] In the event these contingents may never have left home: on 3 August, on the news of the Armada's dispersal, Buckhurst was ordered to halt his troops. A week later it had become absolutely certain that there would not be an invasion of England that year, and the soldiers and sailors of Sussex could resume their normal lives.[24]

There was doubtless great relief throughout Sussex at the news of the Armada's dispersal. The prospect of a Spanish invasion had struck terror into people's hearts, especially in those parts of the county where anti-Catholic feelings ran high. At Warbleton, an east Sussex parish with a particularly strong puritan ethos, where the unusual names given to children at baptism provide a pointer to prevailing emotions, a boy was christened 'Preserved' on 1 August 1588.[25] Could this have been the parents' (or the curate's) response to the wonderful news that the immediate danger of invasion had passed? What is certain is that, when confirmation came of the Armada's final destruction and the Privy Council decreed a national day of rejoicing, there was widespread willingness to comply. There was a 'ringing day for the Spaniards' at Hastings and a 'triumphing day' at West Tarring, while at Lewes 'at the rejoicing day for the overthrow of the Spanish navy' two barrels of gunpowder were 'spent in shooting of the great pieces in the castle'.[26] What a Hailsham man, looking back on the event six months later, was to call 'the late triumph and thanksgiving for our deliverance from the Spaniards' was a celebration that would long live on in people's memories.[27]

For the people of Sussex the coming of the Armada had been a costly and disruptive business. Mercifully there seems to have been little loss of life—the only known casualty was an East Grinstead tailor accidentally killed during shooting practice [28]—but the military and naval preparations had caused considerable losses of time and money. Apparently even Wealden ironmasters, who might have been expected to profit from the increased demand for guns and ammunition, suffered from the disruption: one alleged that, because he and his workmen had been 'employed in the service of her Majesty' throughout that 'troublesome summer', they had been unable to get in sufficient supplies of charcoal and his furnace had subsequently 'stood still' for lack of fuel.[29] The men of Hastings complained bitterly about the crippling burden of victualling and manning eleven crays, serving as fleet tenders when the Admiral was in the Channel: they petitioned the Privy Council for relief and in due course the inhabitants of Pevensey, Seaford, Winchelsea, and several towns in Kent were ordered to come to their aid.[30] Less fortunate was John Young of Chichester, the owner of the ship commandeered by Howard: his charges as we have seen, were supposed to have been borne by five Sussex towns and the inhabitants of all six rapes, but seven years later he was complaining that he had still not received full reimbursement of his costs—so that Buckhurst had to order a 'general and contributory collection' to be made throughout the county.[31]

The defeat of the 'Invincible' Armada did not mean the end of the threat from Spain: indeed fears of an enemy invasion were to persist until the very end of the century. In 1590 there were rumours that a second armada was on its way: watches were ordered to be kept along the Sussex coast, the trained bands were kept at the alert and the towns of Lewes and Arundel were supplied with powder and match from the Queen's store; but the Deputy Lieutenants were told not to alarm the people and to 'give forth that it is only but to provide against certain pirates' ships consorted together to spoil the sea-coast'.[32] Similar precautions were taken two years later when it was feared that the Spanish and their allies in the French Catholic League might 'do some notable account' on the Isle of Wight or some port in Sussex.[33] In 1595, when it was rumoured that a Spanish force had landed in Cornwall, grave concern was expressed about the state of the shire's defences and especially about the ruinous condition of Chichester's walls.[34] Next year it was the turn of east Sussex to be alarmed, when in March came a rumour that the Spaniards had invaded, burned Eastbourne and Pevensey, and 'could not be stayed'. When the news reached Battle 'there was the greatest hurly-burly, woefullest outcries of people, etc. that ever was in man's memory';[35]

and there may have been a similar panic at Etchingham, where some weeks later the rector was accused of saying 'that if the Spaniards should come it were best to yield to them'.[36] In 1597 the Privy Council, being informed that 'a navy with an army of great power is sailing towards England', ordered all gentlemen of Kent and Sussex then in London to go home and take charge of the trained bands.[37] But the most serious alarm came in 1599: in July there were fears that the Spaniards were planning to capture the Isle of Wight and send galleys into Chichester haven;[38] and early in August some Rye fishermen sailing off the French coast heard news that a fleet of 150 Spanish ships, including 40 galleys, had gathered at 'Groyne'.[39] The news caused a flurry of activity comparable with that of 1588: at one time no fewer than 4000 Sussex infantrymen were ordered to march to Ashford to serve in an army being assembled for the defence of Kent; but by early September all the reports of Spanish activity had finally been proved false and the troops were allowed to go home.[40] That was the last occasion when people were to be disturbed by the news, true or false, that a Spanish armada was approaching. Soon peace was to be made with Spain, and two centuries were to pass before England, once more threatened with invasion (this time from the French), was to hear again the echoes of Drake's cry: 'Look well to the coast of Sussex.'

GLOSSARY

Bill A weapon combining axe and spear; a halberd.

Cray A small trading vessel.

Hundred A subdivision of a county, having its own court.

Privateer A privately owned armed vessel commissioned by the government.

Rampire A rampart.

Rape One of the six districts into which Sussex was divided.

Recusant One who refused to attend his parish church; a Roman Catholic.

Seam A measure of weight, usually 2 cwt.

Tun A cask containing 252 old wine-gallons.

FOOTNOTES

Abbreviations

APC *Acts of the Privy Council.*

Boynton L.Boynton, *The Elizabethan Militia* (1971)

Harl.703 British Library, Harleian MS.703 (Letter-book of Walter Covert)

HMC Historical Manuscripts Commission

Mattingly G.Mattingly, *The Defeat of the Spanish Armada* (Pelican edn. 1962)

SAC *Sussex Archaeological Collections*

SP Public Record Office, State Papers

Town Book L.F.Salzman, ed., *The Town Book of Lewes 1542-1701*, Sussex Record Society (1945-6)

1. Mattingly, 126.
2. J.Gairdner, 'On a contemporary drawing of Brighton in the time of Henry VIII', *Transactions of the Royal Historical Society*, ser. 3, i (1907), 19-31; *Letters and Papers of Henry VIII*, xx(1), no.1245.
3. SP 11/13/7
4. SP 12/91/40; 98/12; Harl.703, f.18.
5. R.Holinshed, *Chronicles*, ed. H.Ellis (1807-8), iv,901.
6. Harl.703, ff.46-7.
7. M.A.Lower, ed., *A Survey of the Coast of Sussex made in 1587* (Lewes 1870).
8. Harl.703, f.31v. Cf. F.Kitchen, 'The ghastly war-flame: fire beacons in Sussex until the mid 17th century', *SAC*, cxxiv (1986), 179-91.
9. *Ibid.*, f.42; *APC*, xiv,246.
10. Harl.703, ff.51-2; R.B.Manning, *Religion and Society in Elizabethan Sussex* (Leicester 1969), 146-7.
11. Harl.703, ff.52-3.
12. J.J.Goring, 'The Fellowship of the Twelve in Elizabethan Lewes', *SAC*, cxix (1981), 157; *Town Book*, 33.
13. East Sussex Record Office, RYE 1/5, f.132; HMC, *Rye*, 87-8; G.J.Mayhew, 'Rye and the defence of the Narrow Seas: a 16th century town at war', *SAC*, cxxii (1984), 119.
14. HMC, *Hatfield*, iii,341; R.F.Dell, ed., *Winchelsea Corporation Records* (Lewes 1963), 24; cf. J.M.Baines, *Historic Hastings* (Hastings 1955), 208-12.

15. *APC*, xvi,61,66-7.
16. *Ibid.*, 201-3.
17. Mattingly, 263-6. Mattingly, using the New Style 'Gregorian' calendar introduced in 1582, dates the Armada's departure 28 May; this account uses the Old Style 'Julian' calendar which England retained until 1751. The N.S. date is obtained by adding ten days.
18. SP 12/212/77.
19. *APC*, xvi,176.
20. *Ibid.*, 184.
21. *Town Book*, 33.
22. Harl.703, ff.53-4.
23. SP 12/213/77.
24. Boynton, 163.
25. N.R.N.Tyacke, 'Popular Puritan mentality in late Elizabethan England', in P.Clark et al., ed., *The English Commonwealth 1547-1640* (Leicester 1979), 90-1; J.J.Goring, *Church and Dissent in Warbleton c.1500-1900* (Warbleton & District History Group, 1980), 7.
26. T.Ross, ed., 'Hastings documents', *SAC*, xxiii (1871), 114; W.J. Pressey, ed., 'The Churchwardens' Accounts of West Tarring', *Sussex Notes and Queries*, viii (1939), 10-11; *Town Book*, 36.
27. West Sussex Record Office, Ep II/5/5.
28. *Calendar of Assize Records: Sussex Indictments, Elizabeth I*, no.1110.
29. J.J.Goring, 'Wealden ironmasters in the age of Elizabeth', in E.W. Ives et al., ed., *Wealth and Power in Tudor England* (1978), 216.
30. *APC*, xviii,12-13.
31. Harl.703, ff.76-7,80.
32. *Ibid.*, ff.58-9,61.
33. *APC*, xxiii,160.
34. Harl.703, ff.78-9; HMC, *Hatfield*, v,323-4.
35. T.W.Horsfield, *History of Sussex* (Lewes 1835), i,533.
36. J.J.Goring, 'The reformation of the ministry in Elizabethan Sussex', *Journal of Ecclesiastical History*, xxxiv (1983), 358.
37. Harl.703, f.109; *APC*, xxviii, 60.
38. SP 12/271/20.
39. HMC, *Rye*, 118-19. Since the rumour originated at La Rochelle it is likely that 'Groyne' refers to the Gironde estuary.
40. Harl.703, f.115; Boynton, 204-5.